Me and My Shadow:

A Book about Light

by Buffy Silverman

Science Content Editor:
Kristi Lew

www.rourkeclassroom.com

J 535.4
535.1
Sil

Science content editor: Kristi Lew
A former high school teacher with a background in biochemistry and more than 10 years of experience in cytogenetic laboratories, Kristi Lew specializes in taking complex scientific information and making it fun and interesting for scientists and non-scientists alike. She is the author of more than 20 science books for children and teachers.

www.rourkeclassroom.com

Photo credits: Cover © Lightvision, LLC, Drawvisuals, Cover logo frog © Eric Pohl, test tube © Sergey Lazarev; Page 5 © Jacek Chabraszewski; Page 7 © Jacek Chabraszewski; Page 9 © BEEE; Page 11 © Monkey Business Images; Page 13 © djgis; Page 15 © Samson Yury; Page 16 and 17 hand © plena, flashlight © Almog Ziv; Page 18 © michaeljung, vectorlib-com; Page 19 © michaeljung, vectorlib-com; Page 21 © Pixel Memoirs;

Editor: Kelli Hicks

My Science Library series produced for Rourke by Blue Door Publishing, Florida

Library of Congress Cataloging-in-Publication Data

Silverman, Buffy.
  Me and my shadow : a book about light / Buffy Silverman.
     p. cm. -- (My science library)
  Includes bibliographical references and index.
  ISBN 978-1-61741-741-2 (Hard cover) (alk. paper)
  ISBN 978-1-61741-943-0 (Soft cover)
  1. Light--Juvenile literature. 2. Shades and shadows--Juvenile literature. I. Title.
  QC360.S543 2012
  535'.4--dc22
                                    2011003897

Rourke Publishing
Printed in China, Voion Industry
  Guangdong Province
042011
042011LP

www.rourkeclassroom.com - rourke@rourkepublishing.com
Post Office Box 643328 Vero Beach, Florida 32964

Table of Contents

What Makes a Shadow?

Walk to the park on a sunny day. Your **shadow** follows you.

When the Sun is in front of you, a shadow forms behind you.

Your body **blocks** the Sun's **light**. The light cannot pass through you. A **dark** shadow forms on the ground.

Your shadow moves as you move.

Light travels in a straight line. It **shines** on this tree. It cannot pass through it. The tree **casts** a shadow.

A tree's shadow is shaped like the tree.

Light: Inside and Out

You need light to see. In the day, the Sun lights the sky. Inside your home, rays shine through windows. Light passes through clear glass.

On a sunny day, you don't need to turn on lights.

Close the blinds and the room darkens. Light cannot pass through the blinds.

Many materials block light. Wood and cloth block light.

13

At night, it is dark. You turn on a lamp to see indoors.

A lamp lights the pages of a book. You cannot see the book without light.

Changing Shadows

Shine a flashlight on one hand. Your hand blocks light. It casts a shadow on the wall. Move the flashlight and the shadow moves.

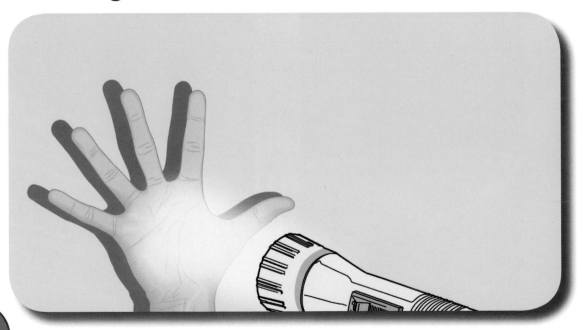

Move your hand close to the flashlight. The shadow grows. Your hand covers more of the light.

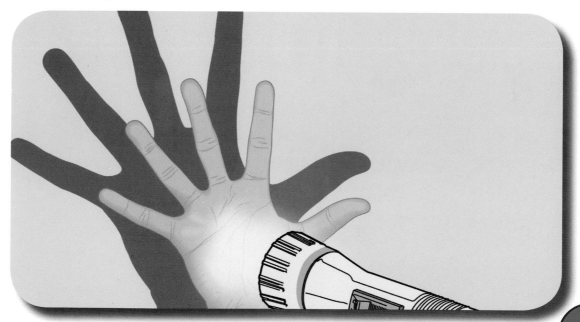

Shadows change outside, too. They move during the day. They grow short and then long.

The Sun is high in the sky. Look at the short shadow.

Later in the day, the Sun appears lower in the sky. Long shadows form.

Shadows are easy to spot on a bright, sunny day. How many shadows can you find?

SHOW What You Know

1. How does a shadow form?

2. Can you name an object that light shines through?

3. Why do we need light?

Glossary

blocks (BLOKZ): to stop something from getting past

casts (KASTZ): to make a shadow appear

dark (DARK): without light

light (LITE): brightness from the Sun or a lamp that makes it possible to see

shadow (SHAD-oh): dark shape made by an object that blocks light

shines (SHINEZ): to give off light

Index

Websites

www.bbc.co.uk/schools/scienceclips/ages/5_6/light_dark.shtml

www.pbskids.org/zoom/activities/do/shadowanimals.html

www.primarygamesarena.com

www.sciencekids.co.nz/gamesactivities/lightshadows.html

About the Author

Buffy Silverman's shadow follows her when she hikes through fields near her home in Michigan. She writes about nature and science.

GUNNISON COUNTY LIBRARY DISTRICT

Ann Zugelder Library

307 N. Wisconsin Gunnison, CO 81230

970 641 3485

WWW.gunnisoncountylibraries.org

24

Comprehension & Extension:

- Summarize:

  What is a shadow?
  Can you name some sources of light?

- Text to Self Connection:

  Have you ever made shadows on the wall using your hands (shadow puppets)?
  What animals can you make?

- Extension:

  Compare and contrast things associated with light and things associated with the dark.

Sight Words I Used:

on
the
through
you
your

Vocabulary Check:

Use glossary words in a sentence.

Forces, Energy, and Motion

Have you ever wondered about the science all around us? Plants grow and change, the Sun rises to warm the Earth, and matter changes from one form to another. Investigate Life, Physical, Earth, and Technology science topics with Rourke's *My Science Library*. This library explores NSTA science standards with engaging text and colorful images to support readers from kindergarten to third grade. Are you ready to investigate?

Books in *My Science Library*:

Animal Adaptations

Animal Habitats

Earth's Changing Surface

Floating and Sinking

I Use a Mouse

Living or Nonliving?

Magnet Power

Matter Comes in All Shapes

Me and My Shadow: A Book about Light

Plant Adaptations

Plant Life Cycles

What's the Weather Like Today?

ISBN 978-1-61741-943-0

90000

9 781617 419430

Printed in China

ROURKE CLASSROOM

www.rourkeclassroom.com